The
White Squirrels
of North Carolina

DON WEISER

The White Squirrels of North Carolina

Copyright © 2005 Don Weiser

PUBLISHED BY
White Squirrel Art Publishing
129 Campbell Drive
Pisgah Forest, NC 28768
www.whitesquirrelart.com

ISBN 0-9773616-0-8

Printed and bound in Canada

My book is dedicated to the beautiful snow white squirrels who visited and amused me these past years ... and with special appreciation to the following people:

My late wife, Beth, for her love and intelligence, none of this would have been possible without her,

My late mother, Ella, for all she taught me,

My lovely daughter, Michele, who also taught me many things, some of which I am still learning,

My wildlife artist brother, Fred, for all his assistance, both artistic and practical, over the years,

My sister-in-law, Barb, for being the first one to spot Whitey, and

My late friend, Reece Cuddeback, who always fed, photographed, and loved the animals.

INTRODUCTION

Visitors to Brevard, North Carolina, often wish to sneak a peek at one of the now-famous White Squirrels. Disbelievers are soon convinced that these critters are truly white (and not just an albino variety). Close inspection (if you are so lucky) reveals that the Brevard White Squirrels have dark eyes like other squirrels. Their coats are truly white by nature's design.

The Legend of the White Squirrel

ACCORDING TO BREVARD RESIDENT, Mrs. W. E. Mull, the legend of the snowy critter's origin goes like this:

> In 1949 a carnival truck overturned near the home of Mr. Black of Madison, Florida, apparently freeing several white squirrels. When Mr. Black observed the unique critters playing in his pecan grove, he caught a pair, and gave them to Mr. H. H. Mull (Mrs. Mull's brother-in-law).

H.H. Mull gave the pair of squirrels to his niece, Barbara, who unsuccessfully attempted to breed them. When Barbara married in 1951, she returned the squirrels to H.H. After one of the squirrels escaped, H.H. released the other, and the squirrels began to multiply in the wild.

Over time the White Squirrels became more than a novelty. Prized by the residents of Transylvania County, in 1986 the Brevard City Council unanimously approved an ordinance protecting all squirrels in the area. The ordinance states, "The entire area embraced within the corporate limits of the city hereby designated as a sanctuary for all species of squirrel (family *Sciuriadae*), in particular the Brevard White Squirrel. It shall be unlawful for any person to hunt, kill, trap, or otherwise take any protected squirrels within the city by this section."

TODAY, THE SQUIRRELS THRIVE IN THE AREA. It's not difficult to observe several White Squirrels playing in the trees or a friendly backyard during an afternoon drive around town.

Brevard honors its White Squirrels by hosting an annual White Squirrel Festival during the last weekend in May — and you're all invited! On the Internet, information about the Festival can be located at www.whitesquirrelfestival.com/

A few other towns across the United States (and Canada) also have White Squirrels. You can find information about them at www.roadsideamerica.com/set/squirrels.html

How This Book Came To Be

WRITER AND PHOTOGRAPHER DON WEISER first saw White Squirrels on the Brevard College campus and immediately became enamored over the critters. (Though reputed to be quite intelligent, no White Squirrels have been known to graduate — yet.)

Several years ago Don's brother, Fred (an accomplished wildlife artist), and sister-in-law, Barbara, were visiting from their home in Tennessee. Barbara was admiring the woods around Don's house when she saw a flash of white flying through the trees.

"Donny, come here quick! Is that a White Squirrel?" she asked.

It was indeed the very first White Squirrel to grace Don's property in Pisgah Forest (or at least the first that anyone had seen). In Brevard, White Squirrels account for 25% of the total squirrel population (they're actually counted twice a year), but until this sighting, White Squirrels in Pisgah Forest were a rarity.

Thinking that Don would enjoy seeing and hearing birds outside his home, Fred had previously suggested that Don put out some bird feeders. It was those feeders that attracted the White Squirrels (now affectionately dubbed "Whitey") to Don's backyard. All squirrels love the black oil sunflower seeds that were in those bird feeders.

The White Squirrel that Barbara first saw still frequents Don's back-yard, and has been named, "Mama" (and sometimes also "Scampers"). Mama will come to Don's deck when those names are called (providing she's in earshot and hungry). Most of the photos in this book are of Mama, but Don is lucky enough to now have four of these rare and beautiful creatures visiting his backwoods yard and deck.

THE PHOTOS IN THIS BOOK were taken with an Olympus C-750 digital camera, 4 mega-pixels, 10X optical zoom.

Don Weiser also produces white squirrel note cards, holiday note cards, postcards, prints, and DVDs of the white squirrels with babbling brooks as background music.

Don's White Squirrel web site: www.whitesquirrelart.com
Don's personal web site: www.donweiser.com

SOME INTERESTING WEB SITES you may want to visit if you have time:

Brother Fred's web site of his wonderful paintings: www.cadescoveart.com/

Barb and Fred's good friends, Wes and Rachelle's (highly accomplished miniature artist/painter couple—they're actually quite tall; their art, however, is miniature sized) web site: www.artofwildlife.com/

One of Don's squirrel rehab friends, Christy's web site: www.wnc-rehab.org/

Don's friend Kaaren's (a decorative artist) web site: www.kaarenpoole.com/index_body.htm

And this tribute web site to a man I never knew, Bill Cooper, who loved his squirrels dearly (this one's required visiting): www.lfwildlife.org/cooper.html

Whitey's
Mountain Laurel
Sojourn

Whitey
Visits the Deck
in Summer

With

Backyard

Birds

Posing
for the
Camera

Whitey Enjoys the Winter too

Whitey
in Natural
Surroundings

ABOUT THE AUTHOR

Don Weiser was born in New Haven, Connecticut in 1945, so he's basically as old as dirt. He grew up (an ongoing process) in the Catskill Mountains of upstate New York, and has a degree in Philosophy. Don is blessed with a beautiful daughter, Michele, from his first marriage to Carol. He left his job and friends in Albany, New York and moved to North Carolina where he and Beth were married in 1990. They lived together in happiness until 1995, when Beth died suddenly at the age of 44.

In 1996 Don moved to Raleigh to start his life anew. "It's off to a somewhat slow start", he says, but we think that's how he prefers it.

Don retired in 1998, and in 1999 moved to the beautiful mountains of western North Carolina where he lives today. He has two indoor cats who think of him as their personal kitty litter attendant. He also plays the Theremin. (Badly.)

Don's modest house is surrounded by woods of mountain laurel, rhododendron, oak, pine, and two small babbling brooks that make beautiful music. Don likes to pretend he's a recluse and a hermit, and perhaps he is. People who have been around Don are pleased that he has chosen the solitary path. Don also likes to pretend he's a photographer and a writer, and perhaps he is some of those things, too. His backyard was recently certified as a "Backyard Wildlife Habitat" by the National Wildlife Federation.

Don has previously published a book he wrote titled, *REWARD, Lost Cat, The Search for Spock*, about how to get back a lost pet and what steps to take to prevent the pet from becoming lost in the first place. Since Beth got Spock (an Abyssinian cat) for Don, it's also a story of how two people living in different states meet, fall in love, marry, and live happily. Don wanted it mentioned he has two other books "in the works". One is a White Squirrel children's book and the other is a photo book of the other wonders such as waterfalls, flowers, and fauna in Transylvania County, North Carolina.